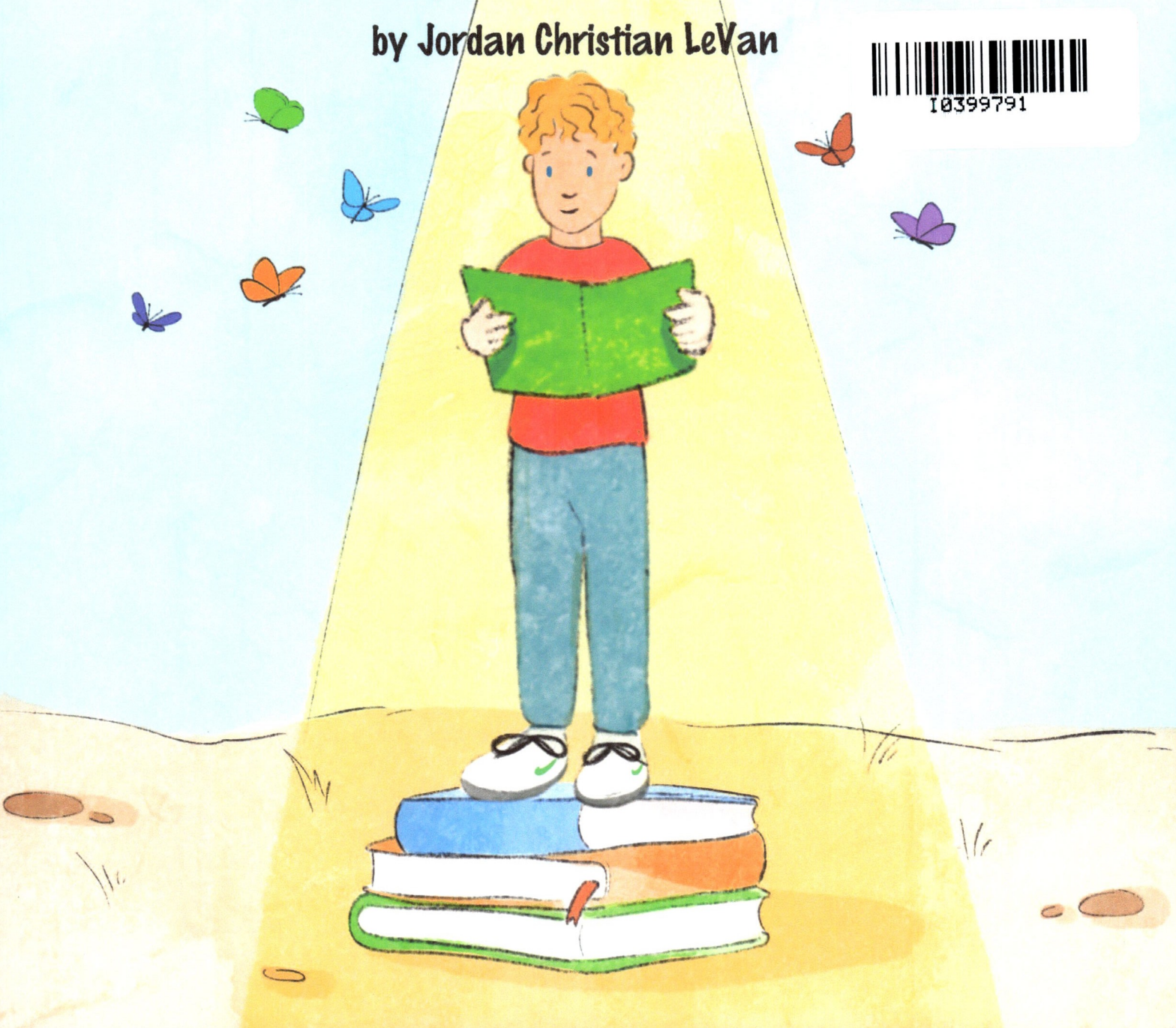

Copyright © 2023 by Jordan Christian LeVan

All rights reserved. Printed in the United States of America.
No part of this book may be used or reproduced in any way without written permission, except as brief quotes included in critical articles or reviews.

For more information visit: www.fightingformyvoice.com
Facebook.com/fightingformyvoice

ISBN: 978-1-7371555-5-3

Jordan's World
The Boy Who Spoke Even When His Voice Shook
by Jordan Christian LeVan

Author Biography

Jordan Christian LeVan is an apraxia, disability, and mental health advocate. He graduated in the year 2020 with his Bachelor of Arts in Psychology, focusing on Mental Health, from Guilford College in Greensboro, North Carolina. Jordan runs a blog called *Fighting for my Voice: My Life with Verbal Apraxia,* where he gives people an inside view on what it's like to live with Verbal Apraxia. Jordan is not only an author and advocate, but he is also the Founder and President of *The Apraxia Foundation: Hearing All Voices, Inc.* Jordan's mission is to create a more inclusive world and to teach everyone that it's okay to be different.

Fightingformyvoice.com

Facebook.com/fightingformyvoice

Acknowledgments

Author: Jordan Christian LeVan
Editor: Lindsay LeVan Towsend
Illustrator: Karine Makartichan

Welcome to *Jordan's World*, a non-fiction book series with stories of my life as a child in the form of art. We're traveling back to the first time I felt confident in my voice. I struggled with self-confidence a lot growing up, but I want you to remember, as I learned– your voice never has and never will be a mistake. I want to thank my mom for advocating for me as a child. I can't wait for her stories to be told. I love you. Let's continue, or should I say persevere?

There are many stories left to be told about a boy named Jordan who had trouble speaking on his own.

Jordan began speech therapy the summer after last autumn's war.
He was so excited about what this season had in store.

The school building was made of bricks and seemed miles wide. Although Jordan was scared, he grabbed his mom's hand and went inside.

As he entered the library, he met his summer speech therapist. She greeted them and smiled. She couldn't understand what Jordan was trying to say.

The speech therapist asked Jordan to find a book to read while she spoke to his mom. He looked over the books, confused, wishing he could read them. The pictures would have to do for now.

While he flipped through the pages, Jordan heard his mom and speech therapist talking. The speech therapist told his mom she was surprised at how severe his apraxia was.

This was the typical conversation that Jordan wasn't meant to hear. However, little did everyone know that Jordan was born to persevere.

Jordan was ready to learn how to read. He joined forces with his speech therapist over the humid months. They played his favorite board games encouraging Jordan to participate and play.

He looked forward to these days because he had fun and made speech gains. Jordan's apraxia didn't always allow him to express what he wanted to say.

The speech therapist was kind and gave him the time he needed to speak. This showed Jordan that she cared about what he had to say.

The summer ended, and Jordan was entering third grade.
He was anxious because his last teacher didn't treat him so fairly.
He didn't want to go, but his mom told him it would be okay.

The new classroom was bigger and brighter, and things were changing for the better. Jordan was finally getting the speech services that he needed.

He started going to speech therapy five times a week. Every day the new speech therapist would continue to help Jordan on his journey to reading.

Jordan had to learn how to pronounce the words before he could read them. This was an obstacle because his apraxia made it hard.

After his mom's advocation, Jordan wanted to read a book in front of the class. He bravely walked to the board and started to speak, even though his voice shook.

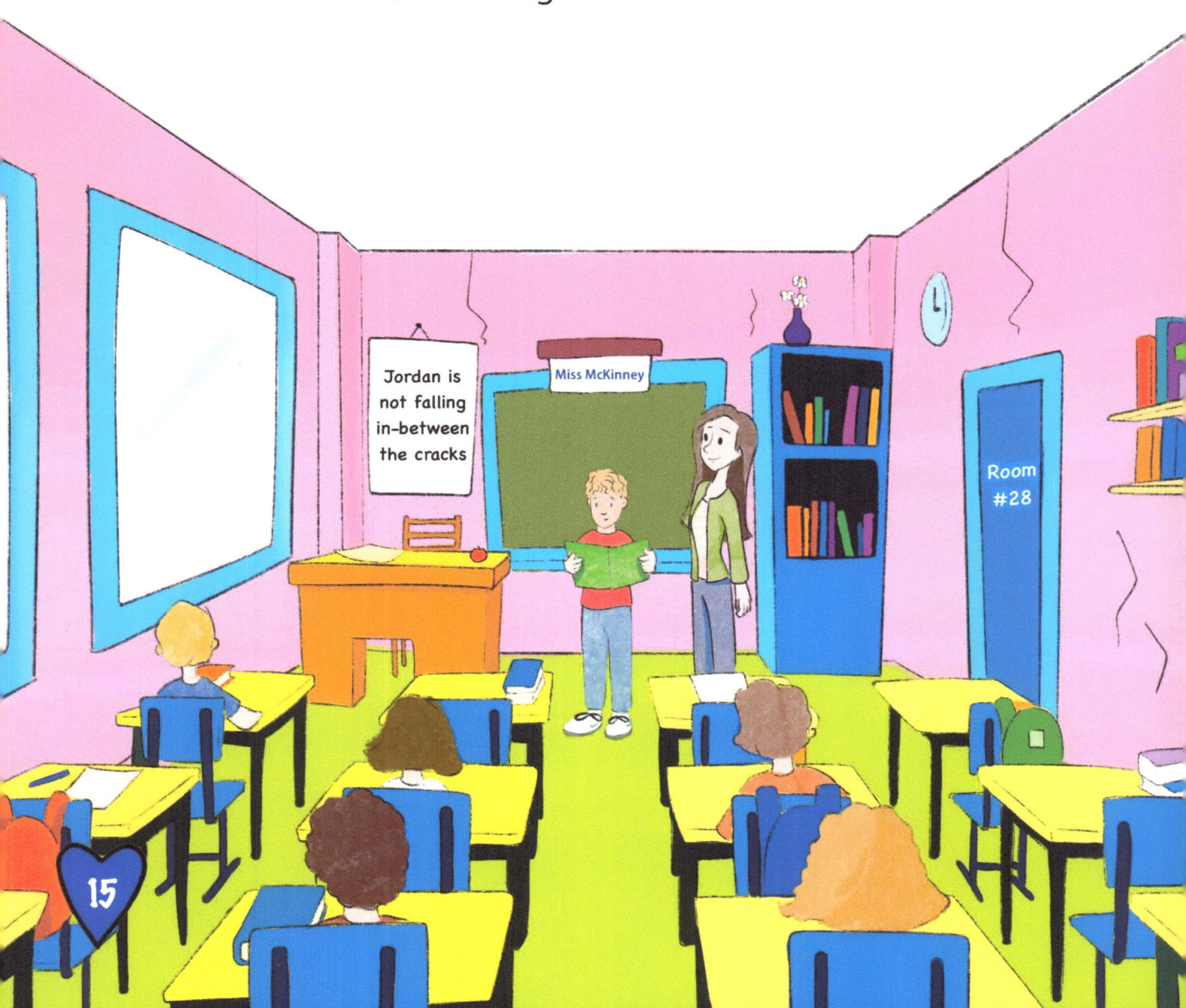

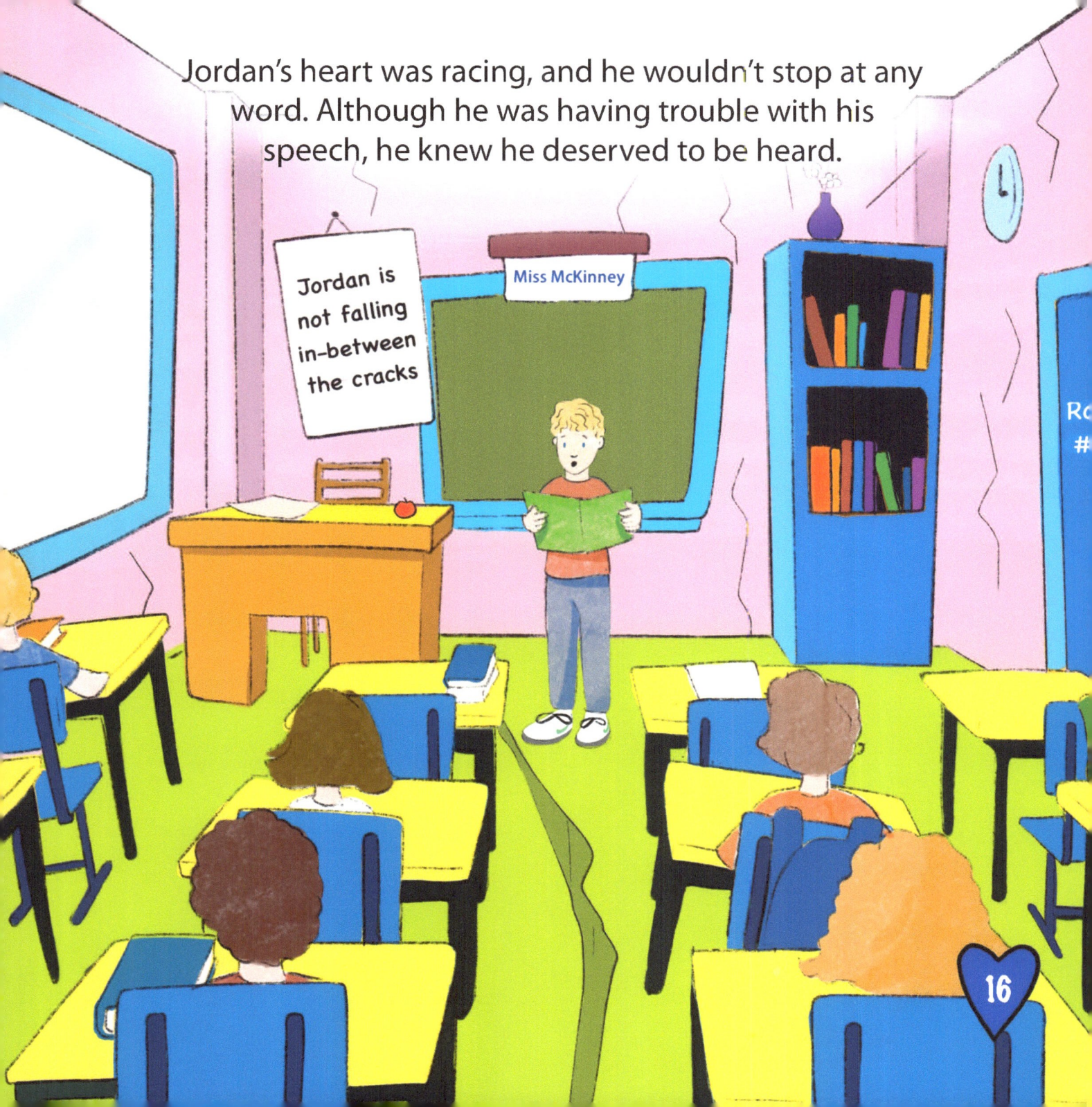

When he finished, he took a bow and looked up to see tears streaming down his mother's face. The teacher did the same with a smiling face.

He started reading more in class, and even though kids like Macy and Hannah would laugh, his voice could now drown out their attacks.

Jordan learned speaking differently is okay, and his words mattered even if they sounded another way.
How you speak doesn't matter;
It's about what you say.

Jordan grew up and taught other kids with apraxia that their voice is not a mistake. In the face of adversity, celebrate who you are. Diversity is a beautiful thing.

Each word you say is a victory within itself, and as Jordan learned this, he found that he was a warrior within himself.

A Letter From Jordan:

Dear apraxia warriors,
If you're reading this, I hope you enjoyed this book about the first time I felt confident in my voice. I want to share some words with you that no one ever told me growing up. Although some people may laugh at others' differences, like speech, it doesn't mean anything is wrong with you. People fear what's different, but that doesn't mean you need to change. Please stay true to who you are. Growing up, I thought my verbal apraxia meant something was wrong with me. However, as I learned, there is nothing wrong with how you were created. You are more powerful than anyone's laugh, smirks, or words. I want you to speak even when your voice shakes because you deserve to be celebrated for who you are. You will get through this, I promise you. Never give up.
I love you.
Love,
Jordan Christian

Thank you for going with me on another trip to *Jordan's World*.
I hope you, too, can find confidence in your voice. We all have things we struggle with, things that make us different, but that does not mean those things are bad. You were never a mistake. You are worthy of being celebrated for the person you are. The next page is a surprise gift for you. You will need a trusted adult's help.
Much Love,
Jordan Christian

Jordan's World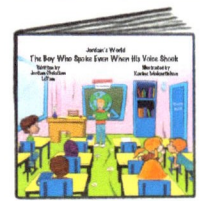

CERTIFICATE OF RECOGNITION

Given To

_____

for fighting for their voice.

Image of the Honoree

Official Fighting For My Voice Member

"I am worthy of being celebrated."

Jordan Christian

Positive Self-Affirmations by Jordan's World

With a trusted adult's help, cut out these 30 positive self-affirmations and put them all in a jar or a box. Each day of the week, pick a positive self-affirmation at random. Carry it in your pocket or bookbag. When you get frustrated, repeat the phrase on the piece of paper and remember that who you are is no mistake. You are amazing, just the way you are.

I am worthy.	I am capable of doing hard things.	I am strong.	I am kind.	I am brave.
I am resilient.	I am determined.	I am enough.	I am perfect the way I am.	I am driven.
I am fighting for my voice.	I am unstoppable.	I am unique.	I am happy to be here.	I am a warrior.
I am proud of who I am.	I am loveable.	I am a survivor.	I am patient.	I am smart.
I am fearless.	I am confident.	I am a powerhouse.	I am successful.	I am "me."
I am everything.	I am brilliant.	I am limitless.	I am capable.	I am courageous.

www.ingramcontent.com/pod-product-compliance
Lightning Source LLC
Chambersburg PA
CBHW041126130526
44590CB00054B/51